John Wesley

Sam Wellman

Illustrated by
Ken Landgraf

BARBOUR
PUBLISHING, INC.
Uhrichsville, Ohio

ISBN 1-57748-722-2

Published by Barbour Publishing, Inc., P.O. Box 719, Uhrichsville, Ohio 44683 http://www.barbourbooks.com

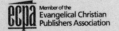

Member of the
Evangelical Christian
Publishers Association

Printed in the United States of America.

John Wesley

"AT LAST," JOHN MURMURED HAPPILY.

1

In Epworth, England, 1709, the February night was a shivery one. Yet five-year-old John Wesley felt warm and safe inside the rectory.

The moment the nursemaid finished wiping John's face, he did not slip inside the curtain that surrounded the bed where he and baby brother Charles slept; instead he tiptoed from the nursery into the hall. "At last," he murmured happily. The nursemaid was too busy to notice. She still had to wash John's sisters: Patty, then Anne, then Hetty, then Mary. By the time they were all ready for bed, John would be back.

John tiptoed down the hall toward a voice, his sister Emily saying, "If only I had some decent clothes,

I know I could work in the house of a rich family taking care of the children. . . ."

"And you would meet a fine young gentleman for sure," gushed his sister Sukey.

John quietly entered the bedroom shared by his oldest sisters Emily and Sukey. In the golden lantern light they brushed each other's hair every evening, while staring at each other in the mirror and sharing stories. John slipped down behind the bed, out of sight.

"Surely Father can spare a few pennies for me," grumbled Emily, "if he can send Sammy to London to a fine school like Westminster."

"Oh, surely," agreed Sukey. "How much money do you think Father makes as the rector of Epworth?"

"I don't speculate how much he makes," sniffed Emily curtly.

"I know how much he makes," giggled Emily, enjoying the joke on her younger sister.

"You devil," laughed Sukey. John heard her gently slap Emily on the shoulder. "How much then?" persisted Sukey.

"HOW MUCH MONEY DO YOU THINK FATHER MAKES?"

Emily whispered something John couldn't hear, then burst out, "That's quite enough to buy me a dress or two!"

The sisters were quiet. John soaked up the golden silence. It was wonderful when his sisters talked, and it was wonderful when they didn't talk. When they were momentarily silent, he had time to chew on what they had already said. Oh, he already knew their father was a rector, a minister of the Church of England. He knew his family lived in the rectory of the church, and he knew his older brother Sammy went to school in London. But he had never thought about how much money his father made. And then he realized with a shock that his sisters, when they were alone, did not address each other "sister this" and "sister that." They were supposed to always do that! Should he scold them? The urge was overpowering.

He stood up. "Sister Emily. Sister Sukey. Pray, let me remind you that you are supposed. . ."

"Master John Wesley!" A hand crunched down on his shoulder.

"MASTER JOHN WESLEY!"

JOHN WESLEY

"Mother!"

"What are you doing in here?" demanded their mother, sticking her head in the door.

"Listening, Mother."

"Bend over that bed, Master John," said his mother. "Give me your brush, Miss Emily."

John rose and bent over the bed, knowing all too well what was next. He felt the dull pain once, twice, three times.

The spanking was over, but not the pain. The pain rose from a dull ache to a sharp stinging. A complaint would bring more pain. He gritted his teeth.

"And me just one month from giving birth to a child," said his mother, sounding winded. "If you can't be trusted to say your prayers in your room, Master John, you will do them for me right now. Stand up!"

John recited the Lord's Prayer. He could not remember the time when he didn't know it. Then he said a prayer for Mother and Father. Those prayers were easy to remember, too. It was a good thing, too, because pain prickled his bottom.

JOHN RECITED THE LORD'S PRAYER.

"Finish this Article of the Church, Master John: 'No man's will is forced...'"

John gulped and finished it: "'...his sin is his own.'"

"That seems particularly appropriate tonight! Now recite some Scripture, Master John."

"'Honor your father and your mother, as the Lord your God has commanded you,'" he said brightly.

"Now off to bed, sir!"

From the height of the second-floor nursery, the cold, dank pools of water and canals called the Fens stretched outside as far as the eye could see. John shivered, because he knew what he had done for several nights was wrong, a sin. It hadn't seemed so at the time. He had learned a lot from his older sisters, especially Emily—maybe as much as he did during the rest of the day.

In spite of the sleep that tugged at him, he dwelled on how he spent every day. Every minute of every day was planned in the Wesley family. Each day John arose only when the nursemaid gave him permission,

HE DWELLED ON HOW HE SPENT EVERY DAY.

and then he said the Lord's Prayer, then prayed for his family, then recited something memorized from the Book of Common Prayer, then recited some Scripture, just as he did at night before bed. Then he dressed and hurried downstairs to breakfast. He sat at a small table with Charles, Patty, and Anne. All the others sat at the large table. His father Samuel Wesley said grace until John's stomach growled. Not one of the six sisters and two brothers talked out loud at the table, unless asked to speak by their father or mother. If John ate his portion and wanted something more, like bread, he silently motioned a maid over.

"Pray give me bread, madam," he would whisper.

After the meal, the toddlers Charles and Patty disappeared to the nursery, and the rest of the children gathered in the parlor, where their mother, Susanna, taught them Latin, mathematics, geography, and history. (Like every Wesley child before him, John had been reading since his fifth birthday. Only Holy Scripture, however, was suitable for learning to read.) At noon, they stopped studying to eat lunch and rest.

"PRAY GIVE ME BREAD, MADAM."

Then from two to five they studied again. As they grew older, their studies expanded into Hebrew and Greek with Father in the evenings.

"And no Wesley child neglects poetry and music," muttered John sleepily. "An educated person can discuss a sonnet or a sonata as easily as the weather."

After supper, they retired to their rooms to be dressed in night robes and washed for bed by their nursemaid. Every moment of every day was intended for some good purpose.

John could see now he had sinned by sneaking out of the nursery. But he was tired, too. Rarely had he stayed awake so long. It must be guilt—yes, the devil himself—that robbed him of sleep this night. He lay in bed and kept thinking of how he had sinned. Perhaps the devil had somehow tempted John, but he had sinned of his own free will just as the Article so wisely stated.

Finally John fell asleep.

THEIR STUDIES INCLUDED HEBREW AND GREEK.

THE ROOM GLOWED AN EERIE PINK.

2

John awoke very tired. The curtains around the bed had the soft glow of dawn on them. But why was he so tired? Usually he couldn't wait to bounce out of bed.

He called to the nursemaid, "Pray, if it please you, madam, I wish to arise now."

And where was babbly, happy Charles? Finding him gone was most unusual. How long should John wait for the nursemaid's answer? He wished to look out of the curtains. But would that once again plunge him into sin? He called again. No answer. He heard scary noises, like loud gabbling voices of demons. He had to look.

The room glowed an eerie pink. Flames danced

across the ceiling! Was he dreaming of hell? He smelled smoke. . . . "Fire!" he screamed, almost choking the words off in fear of sinning. "But I'm the only one in here. Where is everyone?"

He jumped from bed, ran to the door, and opened it. The hall was a red wall of flame.

"Trapped!" he screamed and slammed the door shut. He wanted to crawl under the bed and hide, but he remembered being told to never, never do that in a fire.

John glanced around the room. Flames now splashed the walls. Only a window offered safety. "But it's too high!"

A dresser stood next to the window. He pulled out drawers and climbed them like a ladder, praying the dresser would not tip over. He reached the level of the window. Yes! In the flickering light of an inferno, he saw faces down in the yard—his sisters, huddled, frightened, their faces an eery orange. He rested one knee on the windowsill and hammered on the panes. His father appeared among his sisters, looking bewildered. John tried to open the window. It was stuck.

HE HAMMERED ON THE WINDOWPANES.

"Oh, please, Lord, let them see me," whimpered John.

John's father Samuel scurried around below as if trying to account for everyone. Soon John saw eyes turn toward his window. His family's faces were cast in blood-red horror. Yes, he was sure now they knew he had been left behind. John hammered on the window. "Up here!" he screamed.

Two men broke loose from the crowd. They ran to a spot below John and disappeared. Suddenly a hand shoved his window open with shattering force. The hand reached in, clamped onto John's arm, and yanked him out so hard he blacked out.

Moments later, he opened his eyes. His head was spinning. Faces jumped before his eyes, all clamoring. Did everyone get out of the inferno? Where was Mother? Where was Charles?

"Master John! Praise God." It was his mother's voice.

"Mother!" John looked into his mother's frightened face, smudged black. "Where is Charles?"

THE HAND CLAMPED ONTO JOHN'S ARM.

"He is safe. Everyone got out. Praise God. You're alive." She hugged him, and he could tell she had thought he was lost.

John noticed his father staring at him in wonder. "John was 'snatched from the fire,' " he said, quoting a verse from the Bible.

Wind blew the flames into a raging torch, so fiery they had to move away. Yet as they watched the burning rectory with hot, flushed faces, the icy wind of the watery Fens bit at their backs. Soon Mother took the sisters and brothers across the village square into Saint Andrew's church. All were now wrapped in blankets. The servants were there, too.

"I'm sorry, Master John," whispered his trembling nursemaid. "I grabbed the babies, Charles and Patty, and called for the rest of you to follow. We had to run down the stairs through flames. Then outside I saw you were not with us. I thought you were lost."

"But I'm here, 'snatched from the fire.' Pray, do not distress yourself. Praise God."

After a while his father came in. "Burned to the

ALL THE CHILDREN WERE WRAPPED IN BLANKETS.

ground. It was all timber and plaster and thatch," he muttered.

"Not the dove coop!" remembered John suddenly.

"No, Master John, only the rectory is gone," said his father softly. "The doves are safe. And the barn and stock survived, too." He sighed. " 'The foxes have holes and the birds of the air have nests, but the children of God have no place to lay their heads.' " Father looked around. "We must find homes for the children as soon as possible."

Of the children, only Emily stayed with their mother Susanna; Emily would help with the baby due in just one month. All the others were dispersed: Hetty and Sukey went to London to stay with Uncle Matthew Wesley. All the others went to live with different neighbors around Epworth. John was left with a farm family.

The grown-ups in that family introduced him almost immediately to their own son, Oliver, John's same age but nearly a head taller. When John realized

JOHN STAYED WITH A FARM FAMILY.

the grown-ups were departing he was shocked. His mother had forbidden him to play with the rough children of Epworth.

He hesitated, then said, "Pray, good friends, I'm not allowed to. . ."

"They ain't listening," growled Oliver, interrupting him. "I hope you wasn't going to say you're too good for the likes of me. Come on outside."

Soon John was alone with the boy in the barn. Oliver had been silent when the grown-ups were there. Now his face reddened. "Well, if it ain't the little Wesley cherub hisself," he snarled.

"Master Oliver, I'll not have you speak that way of the Lord's angels."

"You ain't going to do nothing about it. I'm a Fensman. I don't answer to God or queens or men."

"You will answer to God soon enough, if you don't answer to Queen Anne first!"

Oliver snickered, then studied John as if concocting some evil scheme. Even protected by his close-knit family, John had heard the Fensmen were nasty.

"I'M A FENSMAN."

Some in the crowd around the fire that night were muttering that Fensmen had started the fire. His father's public attacks on sinners were not appreciated. Nor were his visits appreciated when he privately scolded the Fensmen.

Oliver started to circle John. "Let's have a good look at you, Cherub Wesley. Ain't you twinkly eyed, to be sure? A right pointy nose to poke into my business, too." Oliver balled up his fists. To John, they looked like sledgehammers.

"Pray, what do you intend to do, Master Oliver?" asked John.

Oliver growled, "I'm going to blunt that pointy nose of yours!"

"I'M GOING TO BLUNT THAT POINTY NOSE OF YOURS!"

HE NOTICED OLIVER'S FISTS.

3

God help me, prayed John.

At that moment, a farm worker in very dirty clothes walked into the barn. He stopped and studied the two boys. He noticed Oliver's fists. "I don't want the destruction of that dainty little fellow on my conscience. So you take care of him, Oliver, or I'll take care of you."

John was shocked. How could a servant speak that way to Oliver? He had an overpowering urge to scold him. "Sir, I believe you've stepped beyond the bounds of proper. . ."

"Shut up!" snapped Oliver, angry over the warning from the farm worker. "Come with me, you little pest."

During the next days, John learned how small he really was. Oliver had friends, and they, too, were taller than John. As a small boy among the small people in his large family, John had not known how small he was until now. Now he realized that his father was a head shorter than most grown men. And John faced the fact that he must learn how to cope among the boys of the Fens, just as he learned how to cope within his own family.

In the next days, he was shoved and tripped and poked and harassed, but he bore it. Finally the other boys grudgingly accepted him like a small tagalong brother. They took no notice of him unless he pointed out some sin they had committed. But John did this often. He couldn't stop doing it, although it brought him pain every time.

"He's nothing but a small replica of his self-righteous father!" snarled one of the boys.

Every Sunday John's father came for him. Each time they passed the quietly gliding Trent River, his father would recite poetry he had composed about the

JOHN WAS SHOVED AND TRIPPED AND POKED.

river. Minutes later, John would be reunited for a few hours with his family in the great stone church of Saint Andrew. John even had a new red-cheeked baby sister, Kezzy, named after Kezziah, a daughter of Job in the Bible.

In Saint Andrew's, order reigned once again for John. His father Samuel did not deviate one iota from the service set down in the Book of Common Prayer. During the sermon, he blistered the parishioners for their slackness. The fire had not slowed him one bit. It had only tempered his tongue into a harder thrust.

Back on the farm Sunday afternoon, the Fens people grumbled. "Why does Rector Wesley give such a hard sermon?"

They did not observe the rest of the Lord's Day. Instead, the Fens people worked and played as they would have any day.

Soon John became accustomed to talking to servants anytime he felt like it, to playing games on the Lord's Day, to singing crude songs, to scuffling in the dirt, to yelling for more food, and to speaking the

SAMUEL BLISTERED THE PARISHIONERS
FOR THEIR SLACKNESS.

coarse accent of the Fens. He hardened under his soft exterior, for he had been the victim of every prank known to the boys of the Fens. But still he politely pointed out their every sin, even though he was finding it harder to remember just what was sinful and what was not.

Oliver shook his head in wonder at him. "You're stubborn enough to be of the Fens yourself, Cherub Wesley, except you're on the wrong side of almost every issue."

One year later, the entire Wesley family was reunited in their new rectory. Their new home was a handsome two-story building of red brick, roofed with tile. Light glittered off it from over fifty windows. Three chimneys spoke of many cozy fireplaces.

John would seldom be able to talk to the rough boys of the Fens now. His mother would make sure of that. It was odd how he missed them, considering the hard way they teased him. But he had discovered things about himself. He was small to be sure, but he was tough. He could take any amount of teasing, and

THEIR NEW HOME WAS A HANDSOME TWO-STORY BUILDING.

although he felt anger during the teasing, he always remembered the proverb in the Bible that said only a fool shows his anger. And John's anger didn't last. Later, he felt as though he were remembering someone else being mistreated.

Mother Susanna eyed the children sternly. "It took one year to rebuild our home." Her voice was full of determination. "Only the Lord knows how long it will take me to rebuild you into children of God!"

How they studied! Finally, John pleased his mother again. He no longer spoke to servants unless it was a whispered request of some kind. He would not dream of playing games on the Lord's Day. Crude songs were replaced by hymns. He lost every trace of the coarse accent of the Fens. But deep inside he carried bittersweet memories of the rough commoners, so hardened by their life of toil. So perhaps the fire had worked some small miracle in him.

He still sensed discontent among his sisters. One evening, John, now eight, approached Emily. As usual

HOW THEY STUDIED!

Sukey was with her.

"Pray, Sister Emily, tell me what bothers you."

Emily scowled. "Father borrowed a lot of money to rebuild the house. He couldn't manage to make ends meet before the fire; how do you think he will manage now—so deeply in debt?"

"Then, Sister Emily, I won't go off to public school."

"Of course you will," she snapped bitterly. "It will just mean we girls must do with less!"

"But surely, Sister Emily. . ."

"Oh, bother with that 'sister' bit! I'm twenty years old. Just one year younger than Sammy who is now studying at Oxford! And what future do I have, not even having a nice dress? I can't even meet a young gentleman."

John said weakly, "But surely, Sister Emily. . ."

Emily growled, "By the time Sammy leaves Oxford, you will be attending public school. By the time you leave public school for Oxford, brother Charles will be in public school. By the time you leave Oxford,

"PRAYER, SISTER EMILY, TELL ME WHAT BOTHERS YOU."

Charles will be ready for Oxford. Do you know how old I'll be before Charles leaves Oxford?"

"No, Sister Emily."

"Almost forty!" she wailed.

Although his sisters' unhappiness gnawed at his heart, John wanted to tell them they were not so unfortunate. He had seen the dirty-faced, red-knuckled women who labored on farms in the Fens. His sisters knew nothing of really hard life. And then there were all their own dear departed brothers and sisters, six of them lying under stones in the Epworth churchyard. Three more were buried in a churchyard over at South Ormsby. Nine poor babies. Yes, that was hard.

"Praise God for life," was all John could say to his sisters.

"Easy for you to say," grumbled Emily. "You'll soon be off to London, my little squire."

"YOU"LL SOON BE OFF TO LONDON, MY LITTLE SQUIRE."

JOHN AND SAM ARRIVED IN LONDON IN JANUARY, 1714.

4

London was chill the January day of 1714 when ten-year-old John Wesley, in black robe and knee pants, stepped off the stagecoach from Epworth. Big brother Sammy helped John carry his baggage inside Charterhouse School. John had one bed among many in a large room. The next morning he found his knee pants tied in knots.

"How amusing," he chirped merrily as he wrestled the knots loose.

The boys of the Fens had prepared John well for this test. Anger was like fuel to pranksters. He must delight in the mischief.

During Latin prayers in the chapel, the boys next

to John faked getting up and down again and again to lure John into a mistake. His heart was pounding. There seemed not a moment of peace. During Greek grammar, several boys coughed and sneezed and snorted as he recited. John smiled at their rudeness. At lunch John was summoned to the headmaster, who told John sharply he had not sent for him. When John returned to his plate, his bread and slice of cheese were gone.

"What a wonderful trick," he said, grinning.

After a couple of weeks of petty tricks, life became almost normal, if one could regard speaking Latin all day as normal. But John was quick with his studies. And he quickly blended in with all the younger boys. He served the older boys no more or no less than anyone else. He polished shoes, made their beds, and ran risky errands. Many a time he slipped from Charterhouse to race madly to Smithfield Market. "Your reward is continued life, Worm Wesley," sneered the older boy as John, panting, would return with a drink or snack.

SEVERAL BOYS COUGHED AND SNEEZED
AND SNORTED AS HE RECITED.

So the years passed. John became one of the older boys himself. When the time came, he found he didn't enjoy working the younger boys as much as he had thought he would.

John rarely went home. More than ever he realized how isolated Epworth was. The truth was that there were many weeks when one could not reach Epworth on horseback or by stagecoach, but only by boat. John remembered now how often his father slogged about the parish, drenched to the skin. John had thought nothing of that at the time. The way his older sisters talked, one would think his father was cozy in his study all the time, composing poetry. But now John knew they were wrong. Pastoring the Fens was a very hard life. So what if his father spent a few hours in the evening warming his bones and writing poetry?

"On the other hand, my sisters have a hard life compared to mine," he admitted to himself.

John heard few complaints from his sisters at Epworth. Writing of their bitterness was not a step they wished to take with a boy John's age. Their main

JOHN BECAME ONE OF THE OLDER BOYS HIMSELF.

news was the astonishing report that the rectory was haunted! During the nights, the family heard knocking noises, groans, and breaking bottles. The Wesleys' dog only whimpered. John suspected that one of his discontented sisters might have been the "ghost." After all, Brother Charles had just left for Westminster School, where Sammy, a minister of the Church of the England now, was a teacher. Might not another example of special male privilege cause a small rebellion?

The haunting became so familiar, the family gave their ghost a name. "Old Jeffrey," chuckled John.

Yet the more John thought about the haunting, the less amused he was. Might not Satan or one of his demons want to become a source of amusement? If one thought all spirits were friendly or laughable, might not hell lose its horror? John turned it over and over in his mind.

"And the dreadful haunting only pulls me away from my studies," he reprimanded himself.

He forced himself to concentrate on his studies again. He was determined to get to the university at

THE FAMILY HEARD KNOCKING NOISES,
GROANS, AND BREAKING BOTTLES.

Oxford, as father and brother Sammy had. He often visited Westminster so Sammy could tutor him. Charles was also living with Sammy. Whereas John was quiet and serious, Charles hummed tunes and enjoyed himself. John was even-tempered, but Charles could explode in anger, then chatter happily a few seconds later.

Finally, when he was seventeen, John was accepted at Oxford, located about sixty miles west of London. "The golden stone spires and quadrangles seem like paradise," he gushed.

Could John hold his own against the brightest students in England? At his own college, called Christ Church, John studied the Bible and classical literature in three languages besides English. He was such a letter writer now that he spent nearly one full day a week at it. The rest of the time he debated other students, composed poems, read his assigned studies, and discussed what he read. Susanna, his mother, had taught him to never waste a moment. He even went beyond the assigned studies and plowed through heavy

HE OFTEN VISITED WESTMINSTER.

Latin classics. He read everything: ponderous religious tracts, plays, satires, farces, and poetry.

"You can't possibly remember so much reading," objected one exasperated opponent during a debate.

Yet John did hold his own against the brightest students. The scholarly life of the students did not trouble John at all, but their sinful social life shocked him. They justified their behavior by claiming sin was not society's main problem. Attention should be focused on social problems like poverty, not sin.

But John soon realized this attitude was merely an excuse to sin. The only effort the students made to address social ills was to throw loose change at the poor—if the poor happened to be standing near a tavern! So John sought out friends of his own temperate habits.

He soon found himself being invited to nice homes in the London area and meeting proper young ladies. He intently watched the manners of the well-to-do and listened carefully. Being poetic helped, too. And soon, much to his amazement, he was writing

STUDENTS THREW LOOSE CHANGE AT THE POOR.

flirty letters to young ladies he had met. All in all, he became quite a young dandy.

As his graduation from Oxford approached, he agonized over what direction his life should take. Should he become a minister of the church as his father and Sammy had done? Much to his surprise, his father wrote him that he must not aspire to be a minister, but instead simply seek to earn his bread. If he would not minister for the glory of God and the service of his church, he should do something else!

Did John really want to work for the glory of God? He thought about it for a long time.

HE AGONIZED OVER WHAT DIRECTION HIS LIFE SHOULD TAKE.

JOHN DELIVERED SOME HARD SERMONS.

5

"I will indeed become a minister of the Church of England!" he blurted one day in 1724.

The truth had come to John mysteriously: He just suddenly knew he would be a minister like his father, uncompromising and exasperating. But perhaps he could be more tactful than his father. There were those who could apply the whip and still be loved. Wasn't his mother that way?

As a deacon, John ministered at Epworth occasionally. He delivered some hard sermons, and his flock seethed in their pews. "Why didn't the deacon just stick to the liturgy and give a sermon on love?"

they grumbled. So John backed off.

John knew his father expected one of his sons one day to step in and take over the rectory. That way John's mother and remaining sisters at home would not be put out on the street upon their father's death.

At fifty-nine years of age, John's father was well-worn. A small stroke had already crippled his right hand. Still, when John was ordained a full minister of the church, he decided to stay at Oxford. After all, ministers in the church had choices how to work for the glory of God. They could pastor or teach others. John decided to be a teacher—like Sammy.

He investigated the spiritual life with more rigor than ever. He read the devotional classic *The Imitation of Christ* by Thomas á Kempis, and its message concerning God's law in the heart inspired him. He also read William Law's *A Practical Treatise upon Christian Perfection,* which emphasized one cannot be half a Christian but must seek moral perfection through self-denial, humility, and self-control. John even visited William Law, who lived near Oxford, and

JOHN READ *THE IMITATION OF CHRIST*.

talked to him. Next, John read the works of Jeremy Taylor, who recommended much self-examination in order to achieve holiness.

"I must record my most intimate thoughts in a diary," John told himself, then added cautiously, "in my own secret code."

In spite of his quest for holiness, John was certainly no throwback to ancient martyrs. He tried to learn every new dance. He played cards. He loved chess. He mastered billiards. He played tennis. He frequented pubs. He picked berries to make his own wine. He went to horse races. He attended plays. He flirted with young ladies. He moved in a social circle of prominent families. All in all, he was quite the young gentleman, a gentleman who just happened to be a minister.

He delved into science, too. He read books on chemistry, magnetism, and gravity. Deciding that true science upheld religion, because it was only a reflection of the Creator's universe, he put any question of conflict aside.

HE LOVED CHESS.

Father Samuel was blunt. "John, it seems you are becoming one of England's 'fox-hunting ministers.' "

Even when John preached at Epworth, when he was not in the pulpit he rode horses and picked berries and swam and hunted birds—when he was not flirting with young ladies. He had a good life. *Too bad Father never learned how to relax a bit, get some balance between work and leisure, and enjoy the fruits of life,* he reflected.

"John," cautioned his mother Susanna, "aren't you living the life of a country gentleman?"

Even Mother disapproved! Well, he was sure fun-loving brother Charles, who now went to Oxford, too, would not disapprove.

But when John returned to Oxford his brother had been transformed. Charles had started a "Holy Club" of like-minded students who wished not only to study hard, but to pray hard and faithfully attend church. John joined the club.

In addition to the goals Charles set for studying and faithfulness, the club visited prisons and slums

WHEN HE WAS NOT IN THE PULPIT HE RODE HORSES.

beyond the quiet of the university. They raised money to support the poor families of the prisoners. They started a school for the children of the prisoners.

Father Samuel was bursting with joy. "To think I have two sons to whom God has given the grace and courage to war against the devil!"

Some other students hated the righteousness and discipline of the Holy Club. They taunted the members with rhymes:

By rule they eat, by rule they drink,
Do all things else by rule, but think.
Method alone must guide 'em all,
Whence Methodists themselves they call.

The name "Methodist" stuck. Other students considered it an insult. John didn't like the taunt, but he thought living by rules and methods was just fine.

He found himself more and more concerned with the world outside Oxford. He soon discovered that the common people could not understand the rich

THEY STARTED A SUNDAY SCHOOL FOR THE CHILDREN
OF THE PRISONERS.

language of the liturgy. What was a minister to do? The liturgy could not be changed by even one word, let alone be abandoned, that was certain. So John came to the conclusion that commoners must be educated. In the meantime, he would try to find simple words to express himself in his sermon, just so long as they meant exactly what he thought. So he made an effort to use common, easy words that were also pure and proper.

At twenty-eight, John joined a group in London called the Society for Promoting Christian Knowledge. It not only encouraged evangelizing in prisons, but it also relocated debtors from English prisons to colonies in foreign lands. James Oglethorpe was starting a colony for debtors in America, all the way across the Atlantic Ocean. The colony was named Georgia after King George.

John met Cherokees brought from America to London. Intelligence radiated from their dark eyes. What would it be like to go to Oglethorpe's Georgia and bring the noble Indians to Christ?

JOHN MET CHEROKEES BROUGHT FROM AMERICA.

Yet John remained in Oxford, studying, teaching students, too, and occasionally preaching. But his father's death in 1735 forced him to make a decision. Would he remain at Oxford or take over his father's rectory?

Then a third option appeared from the Society for Promoting Christian Knowledge: Would John like to be the chaplain of the city of Savannah in James Oglethorpe's colony of Georgia?

"Surely this means God intends me to pastor the pure, unspoiled Indians in Georgia," John confided to Charles. "Imagine me bringing such noble people to Christ. I'll have to deliberate much on Oglethorpe's offer."

Now thirty-two, John had been brooding over his life at Oxford anyway. It seemed too soft, too easy. What did he really want to do? He set his thoughts on paper. Soon he wrote:

My chief motive to which all the rest
are subordinate is the hope of saving my

HE SET HIS THOUGHTS ON PAPER.

own soul. I hope to learn the true sense of the Gospel of Christ, by preaching it to the heathen. They have no comments to construe away the text, no vain philosophy to corrupt it.

There it was! If he truly wanted holiness, what choice did he have? He must go to America!

HE MUST GO TO AMERICA!

THE MEN SAILED TO AMERICA ABOARD THE *SIMMONDS*.

6

Before sailing to America in October of 1735, John recruited others. Soon he had three other members of the Holy Club going to Georgia, too—including his brother Charles! Charles would be personal secretary to James Oglethorpe.

"I'm stunned," said Charles, who wasn't as enthusiastic about America as John.

The four Oxford men sailed to America aboard the *Simmonds* with James Oglethorpe himself. They had private cabins, unlike most passengers who slept below deck in a large hold.

In all, over one hundred passengers were sailing for America, including twenty-six Moravians. These

Germans practiced a mystical form of Christianity and were rumored to be very pious. John whispered to Charles, "Let us watch these Moravians closely. Just how effective is this mystical form of Christianity?"

The four Oxford men themselves kept busy every waking hour, praying, counseling, and studying the Bible. And John didn't waste the opportunity to learn German from the Moravians.

The four Englishmen often met to discuss what they had done and their plans for the next day. This accountability prevented backsliding. They had a pact: No one did anything without the knowledge of the others. Their pact was so strong that every individual undertaking had to be approved by the others. They had a rigid method for voting on this, and if the vote was a two-to-two tie, the matter was decided by lottery.

John continued to keep his secret diary of everything he did every hour of the day, but now at night he also summarized his day in a journal. For stormy November 23, he entered:

JOHN LEARNED GERMAN FROM THE MORAVIANS.

JOHN WESLEY

*At night I awaked by the tossing of the
ship and roaring of the wind, and plainly
showed I was unfit, for I was unwilling to die.*

His father Samuel had had no fear of dying, even
on his deathbed. But John feared death. And that fear
haunted him. It was further proof to him that he was
still only half a Christian. At times he wondered if he
was fit to instruct others. He knew no one he could ask
for advice.

On January 17, 1736, as the *Simmonds* neared
America, they were met by another storm. John wrote
in his journal:

*About nine the sea broke over us from
stem to stern; burst through the windows of
the state cabin, where three or four of us
were, and covered us all over, though a
bureau sheltered me from the main shock.
About eleven I lay down in the great cabin,
and in a short while fell asleep, although very*

THEY WERE MET BY ANOTHER STORM.

uncertain whether I should wake alive, and much ashamed of my unwillingness to die.

Days later more storms battered the ship. John wrote in his journal:

I went to the Germans. I had long before observed the great seriousness of their. . . meekness, which no injury could move. If they were pushed, struck, or thrown down, they rose again and went away; but no complaint was found in their mouth. There was now an opportunity of trying whether they were delivered from the spirit of fear, as well as from that of pride, anger, and revenge. . . . In the midst of the psalm wherewith their service began, the sea broke over, split the mainsail in pieces, covered the ship, and poured in between the decks, as if the great deep had already swallowed us up. A terrible screaming began among the English. The

JOHN WROTE IN HIS JOURNAL.

*Germans calmly sung on. I asked one of
them afterwards, "(Were) you not afraid?"
He answered, "I thank God, no." I asked,
"But were not your women and children
afraid?" He replied mildly, "No; our women
and children are not afraid to die."*

There it was again: faith so strong that death held
no terror. The English passengers did not have such
strong faith. And worst of all, John did not have it. All
his rigor, all his desire for holiness, all his reason could
not give it to him. And yet all the Moravians had it!

The *Simmonds* survived the storm, despite John's
fears, and on February 5 the ship anchored in the
mouth of the Savannah River. John enthused over
America in his journal:

*The pines, palms, and cedars running in
rows along the shore made an exceedingly
beautiful prospect, especially to us who did
not expect to see the bloom of spring in the*

THE SHIP ANCHORED IN THE MOUTH OF THE SAVANNAH RIVER.

*depth of winter. The clearness of the sky,
the setting sun, the smoothness of the water
conspired to recommend this new world
and prevent our regretting the loss of our
native country.*

John soon met August Spangenberg, the Moravian leader already in America. He asked Spangenberg, "How is it that the youngest Moravian has no fear of death, and I am fearful?"

"My brother, I must first ask you a question. Do you know Jesus Christ?"

"I know He is the Savior of the world."

"True, but do you know He has saved you personally?"

"I do," answered John, but now he knew in his heart he did not know that. He believed that only with his head. Deep inside he did not believe Jesus had died specifically for him: John Wesley. What a crushing realization!

"DO YOU KNOW JESUS CHRIST?"

Savannah was divided into fenced lots fifty feet wide and ninety feet deep. Many houses were the original twenty-four-by-sixteen-foot log houses. But to show just how prosperous the future would be for the town, over one hundred new houses were in view, built of planed wood and painted white. Hugging the river was a small fortress with thick walls and twenty cannons.

"Not so obvious are the five-acre gardens and more distant forty-five-acre farms each family receives from James Oglethorpe," someone told John and Charles. "The most common immigrant to Georgia lives like a rich man!"

On March 7, 1736, John preached his first sermon in Savannah. Nearly one hundred people crowded the church. Most of these families were headed by tradesmen who had failed in England: bakers, cobblers, carpenters, barbers, butchers, bricklayers, and laborers. Most of them had been saved from debtors' prison, yet they were as well dressed as merchants in London.

They do appear quite prosperous, John told himself.

HUGGING THE RIVER WAS A SMALL FORTRESS.

JOHN WESLEY

John himself was in no simple set of clothes. He wore a long black cassock—a robe—overlain by the white ankle-length surplice—a loose robe with shorter, open sleeves. Two hard-starched white collars banded his neck. He rarely wore a wig, but today he met his flock with a white wig of tight curls flowing to his shoulders.

He opened the service with a list of hard-and-fast rules that were upheld by the Church of England everywhere. Was it his imagination that each time he went on to a new rule the faces in the congregation hardened a bit more? All he had stated were the minimum rules for discipline. He shook off the uneasy feeling. Love filled his voice as he preached on Paul's great message of love in 1 Corinthians 13.

Next John set out to meet all seven hundred of his parishioners, just as his father would have done. On March 13, he met one young lady so beautiful she took his breath away. He could barely speak.

"Miss Sophy Hopkey, is it?" he gasped.

HE OPENED THE SERVICE WITH A LIST OF RULES.

SOPHY HOPKEY WAS THE NIECE OF
THE MOST POWERFUL MAN IN SAVANNAH.

7

Sophy Hopkey, only nineteen, was the niece of Thomas Causton, the most powerful man in Savannah besides James Oglethorpe. John realized she badly needed religious instruction. He began instructing Sophy every morning.

The half hour he spent with her was but a small part of his busy day. He rose at four and worked steadily until ten at night, praying, working in his garden, writing letters, visiting settlers in their homes, and, of course, ministering church services morning and evening. He was even compiling a hymnbook. His day was very full. Could he spare a few moments every morning to instruct a young lady?

Am I to deny her the gospel just because she's beautiful? he asked himself.

On March 30 he got astonishing news. Brother Charles was in all kinds of trouble in the new settlement of Frederica, south of Savannah. John rushed there, where he found Charles very sick. He had been denied food by the store keeper. He was sleeping on the floor. Worst of all, he was heartsick.

"The entire settlement is up in arms at me," said Charles. "First, I angered the settlers by insisting they not hunt on Sundays. It is sport. It is not allowed by the Church of England. You know that, John. Oglethorpe supported me—most reluctantly."

"Is that all?"

"It's a mere crumb to the seven-layer cake that fell since then! Two of the wives were quarreling with each other. I put myself in the middle as peacemaker. That made them angry at me. They spread lies about me being a bad person. Now even Oglethorpe has abandoned me."

John set to work at once. For five days he talked

HE WAS SLEEPING ON THE FLOOR.

to James Oglethorpe and the two women. At last the women confessed. In spite of their quarreling, they had worked together to destroy Charles's reputation. Frankly, his righteous correction was not wanted in Frederica.

How well John and Charles knew that resentment. Their father had suffered it for almost fifty years. John smoothed over feelings person by person. The situation began to heal.

Oglethorpe sighed. "We will let bygones be bygones."

John returned to Savannah. In all his days, John had never met such conniving, evil people. In Savannah, John and his Oxford friends missed their beloved Holy Club. They tried to get a few of the most devout to meet once or twice a week.

Soon Charles was in Savannah, too. Frederica had no pastor at all. With the others from Oxford, John took turns going to Frederica to minister.

One settler confronted John there. "I don't like your sermons," he snarled. "All of the other settlers

"I DON'T LIKE YOUR SERMONS," HE SNARLED.

are of like mind, for we won't hear ourselves abused."

So there it was again. How sinners hated righteousness. How they hated correction. Those who hate the Light will hate the person who works to shine it on them. The irony was that John had not come to America to correct the settlers anyway; he had come for the Indians. He approached Oglethorpe.

"It is my understanding, sir, that the Choctaws are a very unspoiled tribe. I wish to go among them and teach them the gospel."

Oglethorpe paled. "Where did you get the idea you would minister to the Indians? I'll give you two reasons why you must not. First, England's enemy, the French, will find you there alone and kill you. Secondly, you are needed here. Is there not sin enough for you here among the English settlers?"

More than enough, John wanted to answer. He was very disappointed. James Oglethorpe wanted no one "meddling" with the Indians. Should John give up on America?

Brother Charles soon did. Oglethorpe let him take

"WHERE DID YOU GET THE IDEA
YOU WOULD MINISTER TO THE INDIANS?"

important papers back to the king in England. That way it didn't seem as though Charles had run away from Georgia.

John decided he himself must stay, but he accompanied Charles to his ship in Charleston. On the way, the brothers almost perished in a small boat, but once again God preserved them. And once again John trembled with fear of death.

After Charles embarked, John visited Frederica again. One of the two wives who had been so troublesome to Charles summoned John to her house. He went, thinking perhaps she had repented. Inside her house she confronted him. "Sir, you have wronged me," she said. She brandished a pistol!

John grabbed her arm. Her other arm swung around to thrust a pair of scissors at him! He intercepted that arm. They wrestled over the weapons. A houseboy heard their struggle and ran for help. Finally, a constable stormed in. After the constable pulled the crazy woman off John, he examined the pistol.

"SIR, YOU HAVE WRONGED ME!"

"Yes, it is loaded," he said. Sickened, John left the house.

In the days that followed, the woman and her friends spread lies about John attacking her. John had to go to James Oglethorpe to demand a trial. How else could he clear his name? Surely such an outrage would reach England. This time it was Oglethorpe who tried for hours and hours to reconcile John with the settlers. Finally, all agreed to maintain utter silence on the matter, as well as to never speak to each other again. John was not satisfied, but he knew he could get nothing better.

He returned to a problem in Savannah, too. Sophy made it clear she wished to marry him. He liked her very much. But did he love her? And should a man who desired holiness as much as he did marry at all? He thought and thought. He seemed to change his mind every day.

Sophy's uncle, Thomas Causton, was blunt. "Sophy is twenty now. She needs a husband. Let him be but an

"SOPHY IS TWENTY NOW. SHE NEEDS A HUSBAND."

honest, good man." He looked at John very directly. "I don't care whether he has any money. I now own three houses. I can give him one. And Sophy has a dowry of her own."

John said nothing to commit himself, but he agonized day after day. He really did like Sophy very much. Yet he also shrank from her. Over and over in his mind rang Saint Paul's instructions to unmarried believers at Corinth: "Are you unmarried? Do not look for a wife." And what about Saint Paul's instructions to the married men? "From now on those who have wives should live as if they had none!" Why then would John be so unfair to a woman as to marry her?

But in another passage Saint Paul said it was all right to marry. John could not make up his mind. Finally he decided he and his Oxford friends must make the decision by voting. Charles was gone, but three of them remained.

One was strongly opposed to John's marrying. The other wanted John to marry Sophy. So once again it was John who had the deciding vote! John sighed.

IT WAS JOHN WHO HAD THE DECIDING VOTE!

"My heart says wait, wait, wait. Do nothing."

"Three votes. And three different opinions," said one of the Oxford friends. "We agreed if there was no majority decision, the decision would be made by lottery."

On one slip of paper John wrote, "Think of marriage no more;" on another slip, "Marry;" and on a third, "Wait." He put the three slips of paper in a hat. He extended the hat to his friend.

"Now let God, the Searcher of all hearts, decide," said John with his own heart pounding.

HE PUT THE THREE SLIPS OF PAPER IN A HAT.

JOHN WAS MET AT THE DOOR BY SOPHY'S AUNT.

8

The friend reached in, pulled out a slip, and read, "It says, 'Think of marriage no more.'"

It was the answer John's head wanted. But he felt like a knife had been driven into his heart. He was sick and angry. What had he done? He had refused such a companion as he never expected to find again, should he live one thousand years twice over. So he could not bring himself to tell Sophy right away that he could never marry. He continued to see her again and again, dodging every hint of marriage thrown his way by Sophy and her family.

Finally, one morning John was met at the door by Sophy's aunt. "We appreciate all the instruction you've given Sophy," she said coldly. "Now Sophy desires you publish the banns of her marriage to Mr. Williamson."

John almost fainted. How had this happened? Williamson didn't even attend church services. Yet it was done. For months and months, John had played around the edge of marriage. Now his torment was over.

But was it? In his diary that day he recorded hourly confusion and heartbreak. He could think of nothing else. He couldn't blot Sophy out even from his prayers. His last entry of the day was:

No such day since I first saw the sun!
Oh, deal tenderly with Thy servant!
Let me not see such another!

In the next days, he could not get Sophy out of his mind. He could not rid himself of the pain in his heart. What would he have done if he had known he would suffer such agony over losing Sophy? Was there still

HE COULD THINK OF NOTHING ELSE.

hope? What if he opposed the marriage? Wasn't he the pastor? Yes, this Williamson was definitely not fit for Sophy. It was John's duty as pastor to prevent a bad marriage. Had his father Samuel ever flinched from his duty? Certainly not. But still John couldn't make up his mind. Yes, he would stop it. No, he must not stop it. Yes, he must stop it. . .

Finally an Oxford friend told him, "Williamson took Miss Sophy over to Purrysburg, South Carolina, to be married." He shrugged. "They were married in the Church of England," as if that settled it once and for all.

"Wait," snapped John, "the banns have not been published yet! I can still get the marriage annulled."

His friend talked him out of it. John would just seem like a sore loser. He fumed over it, though. He couldn't hide his disapproval of the marriage.

That made Sophy's uncle very angry. Among other things, Thomas Causton was the local judge. He called a grand jury and gave them a list of grievances against John Wesley. It was a list of every stern reprimand John

THOMAS CAUSTON WAS THE LOCAL JUDGE.

had ever given the settlers.

John remained calm. "I can not argue with the truth of the list," he told the court. "But I merely enforced the rules of the Church of England." John was glad he explained himself and showed he respected the law.

But he found himself appearing again and again in court answering complaints. Soon he realized the suits were a form of harassment by Sophy's uncle. John could get no work done. So he stopped answering summons for court appearances. When he heard he was going to be arrested, he was alarmed. Oglethorpe was not there to protect him; he was back in England raising money for the colony. Still, John hesitated to flee America. He would look like a criminal.

"Leave America, John!" urged his friends. "Causton will jail you until you rot."

On December 3, 1737, John Wesley, minister of the Church of England, fled Georgia on foot in the dark of night. At Charleston he boarded the *Samuel*.

The voyage back to England was the darkest

JOHN WESLEY FLED GEORGIA ON FOOT.

moment yet of John's life. Nothing cheered him. Each hour his failure in America grew more raw, like an angry boil. A more bitter realization than the loss of Sophy grew. John had lost his faith!

On January 8, 1738, he wrote:

> *By the most infallible of proofs, inward feeling, I am convinced. . . . Of unbelief, having no such faith in Jesus Christ as will prevent my heart from being troubled; which it could not be, if I believed in God and rightly believed also in Him.*

Then a storm tested his faith again. The ship nearly went down in mountain-high seas on the thirteenth. Depressed, he wrote of his failure:

> *I went to America to convert the Indians; but O! who shall convert me? Who, what is he that will deliver me from this evil heart of mischief? I have a fair summer of religion. I*

A STORM TESTED HIS FAITH AGAIN.

can talk well; nay, and believe myself, while
no danger is near; but let death look me in
the face, and my spirit is troubled. . .in a
storm I think, "What if the Gospel be not
true?"

The *Samuel* reached England at the end of January. The voyage had seemed an eternity for John. He journeyed to London, downcast. How would he be received? What news had preceded him? What would Oglethorpe say to him?

First, John saw his brother Charles. His brother seemed to feel no antagonism or anxiety whatever over Georgia.

"Mister Oglethorpe controls the news about his colony very effectively," explained Charles. "America is all roses for all anyone here knows."

To his surprise, John found he was in demand as a preacher around London. People hungered for news about the "New World." John also hungered to preach to Londoners. Surely these well-mannered parishioners

JOHN WAS IN DEMAND AS A PREACHER AROUND LONDON.

would not be offended by John's demands for spiritual perfection.

At Saint John the Evangelist's church he preached very strongly on Paul's message in Second Corinthians: "Therefore, if anyone is in Christ, he is a new creation; the old has gone, the new has come!"

After the service, the pastor of the church said, "What were you hinting at, sir? Surely such stalwarts as our parishioners don't need to change! Pray, don't plan on preaching here again, sir."

The next Sunday, John preached at Saint Andrew's in Holborn on 1 Corinthians 13: "If I give all I possess to the poor and surrender my body to the flames, but have not love, I gain nothing." Here, too, the pastor was alarmed after the service. He had seen anger flare in the faces of his flock. Why was John so hard on them? They were good people. They harmed no one.

"It would really be best if you didn't preach here again," he informed John in a trembling voice.

How much more failure could John endure?

HE HAD SEEN ANGER FLARE IN THE FACES OF HIS FLOCK.

PETER'S FACE GLOWED WITH LIVING FAITH.

9

John was pulled out of his depression by a group of Moravians from Germany who were in London for a while before sailing to America. He talked to them at every opportunity, especially to one sunny individual named Peter Boehler. Peter's face glowed with living faith.

"How is it you have such spiritual peace?" John asked him in German, for Peter knew almost no English.

Peter could not explain how. No matter how John tried to coax it out of him through sound steps of logic, Peter could not explain it. Finally, Peter snapped, "My brother, that philosophy of yours must be purged away!"

"I don't understand."

"Exactly, brother! The peace of God transcends all understanding."

John finally saw his mother Susanna at Salisbury. She was staying with his sister Patty.

By now, four of his sisters had unhappy marriages, including Patty. Emily's husband was a broken man. Sukey had left her husband to drift among her grown children. Hetty lived with Uncle Matthew in London until he died in June of 1737. She reconciled with her drunken husband off and on. Only Anne in Hatfield had a happy marriage. Kezzy remained unmarried, living a searching, spiritual life in the home of a minister.

John continued to preach. And his message remained hard. He was rarely ever invited back. One by one, he was eliminating every pulpit in the London and Oxford areas. What was to become of him?

Meanwhile he sought spiritual advice from Boehler. He could not have such conversations with

JOHN CONTINUED TO PREACH.

Charles, for Charles was having his own doubts. Peter Boehler insisted that someday John would find the powerful faith he was looking for. It would happen suddenly. John would not be able to explain afterwards what had happened. But John was a skeptic. Did that explanation bear examination? He searched the New Testament. Yes, there were many sudden transformations.

Oh, the Moravians were so wise! Peter was a young man, ten years younger than John. Yet he was so wise.

But in the meantime faith eluded John. He was sure he no longer had it. Perhaps he would be inspired by the new society begun in London at Fetter Lane, May 1, 1738, by James Hutton. It was very nearly the image of their old Holy Club at Oxford, but there was one striking difference: It was not just for the privileged. Of the nine original members, only John, Hutton, and John Shaw were educated. The others were all tradesmen and laborers.

John marveled to Charles about the laborer John

FAITH ELUDED JOHN.

Bray. "He knows nothing but Christ, yet by knowing Him, he knows and discerns all things."

"We've been too isolated, brother. Wasn't the tinker John Bunyan even a more brilliant version of how a man who knows only Holy Scripture can know everything important?"

Still John did not find the faith he was searching for. Then Peter Boehler sailed for America, and John became very depressed again. Church after church told him not to preach to their congregations again: Saint Catherine's, Saint Lawrence's, Saint Ann's at Aldersgate, Saint John's at Wapping, Saint Bennet's at Paul's Wharf, and on and on. John was not advancing the faith. He was sinking it!

About this time, Charles, sick in bed, claimed to have a sudden spiritual awakening. One of the Moravians, William Holland, came to his room and preached from Martin Luther's *Commentary on Galatians*. Later that night, Charles could not stop thinking about verses 20 and 21 in Galatians 2:

WILLIAM HOLLAND PREACHED FROM MARTIN LUTHER'S BOOK.

JOHN WESLEY

I have been crucified with Christ and I no longer live, but Christ lives in me. The life I live in the body, I live by faith in the Son of God, who loved me and gave himself for me. I do not set aside the grace of God, for if righteousness could be gained through the law, Christ died for nothing!

That night Charles fell asleep praying, *If only it were true for me, Charles Wesley.*

"And in the morning, John, my prayer was answered," cried Charles. "At last I have rest for my soul. I immediately began to feel healthier, too."

If only that were to come true for me, thought John.

Three days later, he was invited to a society meeting in Aldersgate. He did not want to go, for he was very depressed. No one sought faith harder than he did, yet he was denied faith. He trudged to the meeting, where that same William Holland was reading, this time from Martin Luther's *Preface to Romans.*

HOLLAND WAS READING FROM
MARTIN LUTHER'S *PREFACE TO ROMANS.*

John listened lifelessly. Holland reached the portion describing the change God works in the heart through faith in Christ.

The heart, reflected John analytically, is neither righteous nor evil, but the inner place where the Holy Spirit must dwell—if at all.

Suddenly warmth swelled inside John's chest! His heart seemed to lift him off the floor. His mind soared. He realized he did trust Christ alone for salvation. Christ had died for him: John Wesley. Christ's blood had washed away John Wesley's sins. Christ alone had saved John Wesley from death. And John, who always tried to note every detail, shakily wrote down the time that evening of May 24, 1738: eight-forty-five.

The next morning he awoke with "Jesus, Master" on his lips. "I am sure I am in Christ now, a new creation," he cried. "Life will never be the same. I am sure of that." John was sure he had been reborn. "Somehow I must use what I've learned, even though I'm almost an outcast in my own church. The Moravians had to

JOHN HAD BEEN REBORN.

leave the Lutheran Church. Is that what I must do to establish a living faith? Leave the Church of England?" He recoiled from that. It seemed unthinkable.

In London, John was rarely invited to preach, so he threw himself into visiting jails and workhouses, as well as attending small societies. He and Charles began to consider going back to Oxford to teach.

In March of 1739, John received an invitation from an old friend from Oxford, George Whitefield, to come to Bristol. Whitefield had been back from Georgia since December. He, too, found the pulpits in England closed to his hard message. Now he was doing the unthinkable.

"He is preaching outside of the church," said John to Charles. "Literally."

"What? Outside? Preaching among the trees?" asked Charles, disgusted. "With the clods under his feet as his pulpit?"

"With the sky as his sounding board, brother," continued John, just as disgusted.

"Surely you are not going." Impulsively Charles

JOHN VISITED JAILS AND WORKHOUSES.

grabbed a Bible. Often the brothers accepted as God's will the first verse their eyes fell on when they opened the Bible at random. "Look here, John—Ezekiel 24:16."

Charles read it aloud: " 'With one blow I am about to take away from you the delight of your eyes. Yet do not lament or weep or shed any tears.' "

John's jaw dropped. "It seems you've sent me to Bristol, brother."

THE BROTHERS ACCEPTED AS GOD'S WILL
THE FIRST VERSE THEY SAW.

"I WANT YOU TO CARRY ON MY WORK."

10

So John was off to Bristol! Trade with America had made Bristol the liveliest city in England outside of London. The city bustled with seafaring men, always notorious sinners when in port. George Whitefield had been preaching there as well as to the coal miners of nearby Kingswood.

Whitefield got straight to the point. "John, I want to return to America. I want you to carry on my work."

"What! Preaching outdoors is revolting to me," said John with his usual bluntness.

Whitefield smiled. "I'm sure what you say to me is true. When did you not speak the truth? But I also know you love reason. So let me make my case."

"Proceed," said John skeptically.

"Certain areas of England are booming as never before," explained Whitefield. "Here in Bristol the city happens to be growing because of shipping, and Kingswood is growing because of coal mining. But all over England areas are exploding with new activity and growth. Jethro Tull has changed farming with his seed planters and other inventions. John Kay has revolutionized weaving with his flying shuttle. Machines are being invented for this and that, left and right."

"I'm beginning to see the problem. . ."

"The Church of England is notoriously slow to create new parishes."

"Of course, it takes an act of Parliament."

"So you do see the dilemma, friend. Great numbers of the unchurched are growing. The poorest laborers and farmers among us are unchurched. Someone must do something. And if you and I are not welcome in the pulpits of the churches, perhaps it is God's will that we preach to these unchurched out of the pulpit."

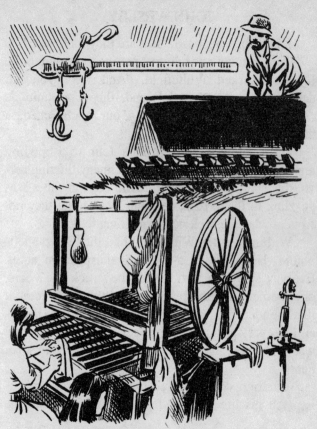

"ALL OVER ENGLAND AREAS ARE EXPLODING WITH NEW ACTIVITY AND GROWTH."

John shook his head. "But are they interested?"

"Did you not once go to America to preach to the Indians?" asked Whitefield. "And were you not denied the opportunity? Friend, the opportunity is right here in England among our unchurched, a thousandfold!"

On April 1, Whitefield took John to a bowling green in Bristol. A crowd gathered, many tittering nervously. The sight of clergymen in solemn robes was puzzling to them, realized John. How could they not wonder what these clerics were going to do?

Within minutes Whitefield had the crowd spellbound. He was like a great Shakespearean actor. Every crisp syllable off his tongue struck one's ears, one moment like the purr of a cat, the next moment like thunder. His voice carried to the farthest listener. His every gesture was perfect. George Whitefield was the most dynamic preacher John had ever heard.

Yet John was sickened by this outdoor preaching. All his life John had gained comfort from the

WHITEFIELD WAS THE MOST DYNAMIC PREACHER
JOHN HAD EVER HEARD.

trappings of the church building. He was such a stickler for order. Everyone knew that. This field preaching was so crude.

"Surely one could not save souls in a bowling green!" muttered John to himself disagreeably.

John continued on with Whitefield to the mine-pitted region of Kingswood, past slag heaps and pitiful shacks. They stopped at a place called Hannam Mount. From that green rise, Whitefield preached again, just as strongly. The crowd seemed hungry for the Word. Some had obviously heard Whitefield before.

The two ministers continued on to Rose Green. Again a crowd gathered, larger than the one before. Whitefield preached again. John's head was spinning. How many thousands had Whitefield reached that day? And what poverty and misery infested Kingswood! What work there was to be done here.

That night John preached to a small society on Nicholas Street. Unlike Whitefield's alternating purrs and thunder, his delivery was constantly graceful and easy. His voice was clear, conversational. Yet he

HOW MANY THOUSANDS HAD WHITEFIELD REACHED THAT DAY?

knew it resonated off the far walls. John was far too methodical not to have learned how to project his voice inside a building. Surely this enclosed safety was his destiny.

That same night Whitefield told him, "I'm supposed to preach tomorrow afternoon—at the brickyard at the end of Saint Phillip's Plain. But I'm leaving for London at dawn."

John was shocked. "Surely you don't expect me to. . ."

"Give it a chance," Whitefield implored John.

The next day—April 2, 1739—John trudged to the brickyard at four o'clock in the afternoon, feeling the fool, stumbling over clods in his elegant cassock. But when he first saw the grimy faces of laborers and their families, his heart ached; they required his utmost effort. And now he realized the extent of the crowd. Thronged on the clay banks were at least three thousand people! John stood on a small rise and preached on the very essence of his own calling now from Luke 4:18: "The Spirit of the

ON THE CLAY BANKS WERE AT LEAST THREE THOUSAND PEOPLE!

Lord is on me, because he has anointed me to preach good news to the poor."

Still, preaching outside makes my skin crawl, he admitted to himself that night.

Yet the next morning he awoke singing a hymn. By the next Sunday he found himself following Whitefield's very footsteps of the previous Sunday. But would anyone show up for the unknown John Wesley?

At the bowling green in Bristol he preached at seven in the morning. Praise the Lord, about one thousand showed up. Then he preached at Hannam Mount in Kingswood—to about fifteen hundred, he guessed. Then he continued on to other side of Kingswood and Rose Green. There in the afternoon he preached to five thousand!

At the end of the day, he realized he had preached to seventy-five hundred people. "How many pulpits would it take to reach that many? And these dear people stand outside in the weather!"

Wonders seemed to come every day now. John had worried he would gradually lose Whitefield's

IN THE AFTERNOON HE PREACHED TO FIVE THOUSAND!

following. But instead, he built on it. One Sunday in early June, John preached to six thousand at Hannam Mount, then eight thousand at Rose Green.

Soon John had made such a commitment to preaching in the Bristol area and he had such a following that he was able to raise money to buy a lot in the Horse Fair near St. James's churchyard. He wanted to build a meetinghouse. Things were happening so fast; the first stone was laid three days later.

"I have incurred a large personal debt myself!" he told his friends, not in complaint but wonder. "But we must have a place to gather. We must do more than preach. We must follow through in Christian living."

Before long he was preaching in the new building as well as his routine outside places. He spoke from a desk facing the crowd that sat on benches in a long room. Off to the side of the long room was a smaller room, intended for school and small meetings. John slept in a tiny room in the loft. A stable in back sheltered horses.

JOHN SPOKE FROM A DESK.

He didn't dare think of this building as a church. Splitting off from the Church of England was unthinkable. If people had to have a name, let them call it the "New Room" for the "Methodist Society."

"Might as well," he said. "The name 'Methodist' sticks to me like a burr."

HE DIDN'T DARE THINK OF THIS BUILDING AS A CHURCH.

THE ENGLISH PEOPLE LOVED TO SING.

11

John learned Whitefield had gone to London and convinced Charles Wesley to preach in the open, too. Soon the brothers were comparing notes on their services.

The Church of England only chanted psalms. Both Wesleys had long thought that was a deficiency. The Bible advocated praise in the form of singing. The Wesleys now introduced spirited hymns.

The English people loved to sing. John translated the very best hymns from French, German, and Spanish into English. Poetic Charles began writing his own. The Wesleys' message in their preaching was hard, but oh, the joy of those hymns!

John began to preach in more places now, even venturing into Wales. Crowds grew. Ten thousand. Fifteen thousand. Twenty thousand. Most were no more than curious at first about this "Methodist" and his hymns. But it brought them to the gospel.

Spreading the gospel far and wide, yet establishing local societies, required the most methodical planning. John Wesley was just the man to do it. But in order to evangelize more widely, he needed someone reliable to hold down the Bristol ministry. Who better than brother Charles?

"Let us hope this turns out better for us than America did," sighed Charles, not thinking to resist.

The Methodists needed a base in London. So John bought an old foundry north of the Thames in the sprawling area called Moorfields. Its enormous rooms were once used for casting metal, but renovation produced a chapel that could hold up to seventeen hundred people. An adjoining chamber was a school room that could hold three hundred pupils.

JOHN BOUGHT AN OLD FOUNDRY.

Over the schoolroom were living quarters. Their mother Susanna was soon living there, then their sister Emily, whose husband had died. The "Foundry" offered prayer services in the morning and at night.

John also started a work program at the Foundry. "The poorest of the poor are given work each day carding and spinning cotton," he wrote Charles.

John was not always there. He was busy field preaching, for there weren't enough field preachers.

Then a crisis arose within the Methodists. John heard that Thomas Maxfield, a Methodist minister not ordained by the Church of England, was preaching in London. That was highly irregular. Should John dismiss him?

His mother took John aside. "I'm the daughter of an Oxford graduate, who was ordained as minister so he could preach. I'm the wife of an Oxford graduate, ordained as minister so he could preach. I'm the mother of three Oxford graduates, all ordained as ministers so they could preach. I've

JOHN STARTED A WORK PROGRAM AT THE FOUNDRY.

heard Thomas Maxfield preach. He is as surely called by God to preach as any of you are!"

John listened to Maxfield preach. His mother was right. And from that day on lay preachers were part of the Methodist societies. But this meant another duty for John, for he must approve the fitness of each and every one. He soon had a set of twelve "rules" for preachers. They were all grounded in Holy Scripture: "Be diligent and work hard," "Be serious," "Talk little, particularly with young women," and "Speak evil of no one" were some of his rules.

His sister Mary and his father had died some years before, but death struck the Wesleys hard in the years from 1739 to 1742. Once a tight, disciplined family of one dozen under the rule of Samuel and Susanna, five had fallen. Now brother Sammy died, only forty-nine years old. Younger sister Kezzy died. And most crushing to John, his mother Susanna died at seventy-two.

BROTHER SAMMY DIED.

In 1742 John, now thirty-nine, rode into Newcastle, the great coal town in the north of England. Never before had the town seemed so wicked to him. "So much drunkenness and swearing—even from the mouths of children—I have never witnessed before," he told his companions. "Surely this place is ripe for Him who 'came not to call the righteous, but sinners to repentance.' "

He realized Newcastle must be the third base for his Methodist organization. There he was anxious to build a "room," his modest description of a community center for worship and school. It would house a chapel, classrooms, a bookshop, living quarters for traveling preachers, even a hospital. He also started another center in London, this one on West Street. His appeal was so great that when he first preached in its chapel, congregations had to be admitted in relays over five hours.

"But not everyone welcomes me," he observed dryly.

JOHN RODE INTO NEWCASTLE.

JOHN WESLEY

The growing popularity of the Methodists alarmed some people so much they tried to harm John. In 1741, a gang ran an ox into John's crowd at Charles Square in London. No one was killed, but John was sickened by the incident. Yet he realized he had no fear for his own safety. At long last he had total trust in God, like the Moravians.

In early 1742 John was tested again. A gang broke into an inside meeting and started ripping the house apart. John faced down the ringleader, who suddenly fell to his knees, struck down by remorse. Just weeks later, a gang drove a bull into the table John was speaking from. Supporters rescued him and carried him away on their shoulders before the table was trampled into splinters. Again John had no fear.

His travels were always dangerous. In Darlington, near Newcastle, both his horse and his companion's horse died when someone poisoned them. Once while preaching, a brick grazed his shoulder.

A GANG RAN AN OX INTO JOHN'S CROWD.

Once a stone struck him between the eyes. Once he got punched in the mouth.

In the village of Wednesbury, he was whisked away in pouring rain by a mob of several hundred. Then another mob met the first one. They scuffled for control of John. Many tried to knock him down. One man whacked at him with a club. His clothes were torn, his hand scraped raw, his mouth bloodied. Finally he was rescued by the mayor of Wednesbury. During the entire ordeal John's fear was utterly gone.

"Praise God," he said.

Just three days later, John pestered ferrymen to take him across the rain-swollen Trent River, not far from Epworth. Finally they did. The barge capsized, with horses and men tumbling into the torrent. Yet the barge would not sink. The astonished ferrymen poled the barge to the other side. All were safe, even those who fell into the river. John could not move. They discovered a large iron crowbar had

THE MOB SCUFFLED FOR CONTROL OF JOHN.

slipped though a loop on his boot, fastening him to a plank of the barge. If the barge had sunk, John would have drowned.

"Praise the Lord. Surely God kept the barge afloat," they all said.

GOD KEPT THE BARGE AFLOAT.

THE LEADERS OF THE METHODIST SOCIETIES
HELD THEIR FIRST CONFERENCE.

12

In the summer of 1744, the leaders of the Methodist societies held their first conference in London. In the meeting were John, Charles, and eight others. The ten leaders first discussed doctrine. What did they mean by justification? Repentance? Saving faith? Sanctification?

"Leaders of our societies shall not use pious phrases that they themselves can not explain," said John. "And we must wherever possible use simple everyday words, just so long as they are pure and proper for the meaning."

The ten men agreed that Methodist preachers would not perform the sacraments of baptism and

Holy Communion. Those could be done only within the Church of England. In fact, no society meetings were ever to take place while a local parish church was holding services. John advised that the basic Methodist service be only half an hour, with one hymn before the sermon and one hymn after. Hymns were so important that the brothers now published their own hymnbooks.

John praised the hymns written by Charles. "I think no one else composes hymns in the English language so full of Scripture."

One only had to hear hymns by Charles like "Jesus, Lover of my Soul" to appreciate their pure poetry:

Jesus, lover of my soul,
Let me to Thy bosom fly,
While the nearer waters roll,
While the tempest still is high:
Hide me, O my Savior, hide,
Till the storm of life is past;

THE BROTHERS NOW PUBLISHED THEIR OWN HYMNBOOKS.

JOHN WESLEY

Safe into the haven guide,
Oh, receive my soul at last!

"Now, gentlemen," said John to the other men, "we've arrived at the heart of the societies, our membership. Has each member lived the gospel?"

John was very tolerant on slight differences in beliefs. After all, weren't all Methodists "fleeing the wrath of God," seeking holiness and perfection? But that tolerance did not stretch to behavior. Any member who did not behave according to the gospel had to depart. And living the gospel had been set down by the Methodists as "General Rules," different from the rules for preachers. The ten leaders went through their entire membership, commenting on how well each member lived the gospel.

As a result, they reduced the membership so much some grew alarmed. "We've cut so many!"

"Numbers are not significant," said John. "May God increase our societies in faith and love."

They even discussed the clothing of their preachers.

"HAS EACH MEMBER LIVED THE GOSPEL?"

The long frock coats and knee pants were cool blues and grays. White shirts and stockings were expected to be clean. Headware was a three-cornered hat. They must never sport silks or satins as dandies did.

They also discussed their "circuits," a network of societies that each of the ten shepherded. It required riding a horse over the rough roads hours each day.

Eventually one of the ten broached a very explosive subject. "Will we Methodists eventually separate from the Church of England?"

"Certainly not, sir!" answered John. "Even after our deaths, our Methodists will remain in the Church of England, unless the church throws them out!" But as he studied their faces he saw that even Charles looked skeptical.

The men agreed to hold a conference every year and returned to their circuits. John promised to put more advice in writing. Even traveling four thousand miles a year now, it was getting harder and harder for him to visit every society. He would issue guidelines for preaching. His duties seemed boundless.

THE LONG FROCK COATS AND KNEE PANTS
WERE COOL BLUES AND GRAYS.

He also worked steadily on his own holiness. John had drunk tea several times a day for twenty-six years, but it was time to surrender it. For three days after he stopped drinking tea he had a headache. The third afternoon he lost his memory. Then his memory crept back. He prayed and prayed. Finally he felt as fit as ever. Tea was beaten.

"The severe effects of my withdrawal only prove how corrupting it was," concluded John.

John was very concerned with health and the treatment of illnesses. In London, he opened a dispensary, employing a pharmacist and a physician. He even worked there himself, being widely read on medicines. Not satisfied with that local effort, he wrote *An Easy and Natural Method of Curing Most Diseases,* a book in which he prescribed 725 prescriptions for 243 diseases. The prescriptions were simple ones that people could easily obtain. He intended to distribute this book to every member of the societies. "Servants for God need to stay healthy," he insisted.

HE EMPLOYED A PHARMACIST AND A PHYSICIAN.

JOHN WESLEY

John needed his own good health, for he pushed himself relentlessly. Nothing stopped him. In February of 1747, he and his companions journeyed north from London, into blowing snow. Soon hail was blasting them so hard they could not see, and they could scarcely breathe. Yet at six that night John preached in Potten, nearly forty miles north of London. The next day they were pelted by sleet, which froze instantly to whatever it struck. They stopped frequently to break out of their encasing ice, then pushed on. At sunset they reached an inn nearly thirty miles from Potten!

The next morning the road was invisible in a sea of white snow. The Methodists dismounted and led their horses through huge dunes of snow. By evening they were twenty miles farther north. John had a toothache so painful he could not speak, but he was no less determined. He tolerated few excuses for not pushing ahead.

Once, stalled at a port, he vented his frustration by composing a ditty:

THE METHODISTS LED THEIR HORSES
THROUGH HUGE DUNES OF SNOW.

JOHN WESLEY

There are, unless my memory fail,
Five causes why we should not sail;
The fog is thick, the wind is high;
It rains, or may do by and by;
Or—any other reason why!

His schedule was staggering. One week in 1747 he preached fifteen times in thirteen different places. He had preached one thousand sermons a year for almost ten years now.

Enthusiasts wanted him to start societies in Ireland and Scotland, too. So in 1748 John began to preach in Ireland. It seemed a fierce country to him. "I fear God still has a controversy with this land," he said. But the Irish were warmhearted, and John could not stay away. Scotland was a different story. The Scots were cool to John and the Methodists.

In Newcastle, John became very ill. A faithful Methodist worker, Grace Murray, nursed him. The widow seemed to know exactly what to do. Her voice was calm and cheerful. He had not felt such an

IN NEWCASTLE, JOHN BECAME VERY ILL.

attraction for a woman since he adored Sophy in America many years before.

He found himself thinking out loud. "If ever I married, Grace, you would be a perfect wife!"

Then to his amazement he learned his brother Charles also wanted to marry. . . .

GRACE WOULD BE THE PERFECT WIFE.

JOHN PERFORMED THE CEREMONY.

13

Naturally, Charles put his reasons to marry in verse:

Two are better than one,
For counsel or for fight!
How can man be warm alone
Or serve his God aright?

So in April of 1749, Charles Wesley, bachelor of forty-one, wed Sally Gwynn, only twenty-two. John performed the ceremony at Garth. Charles took his new wife Sally to Bristol to live. Later, John realized he forgot to tell Charles how he felt about Grace Murray.

John was so busy. In addition to everything else,

he had now perfected an exhaustive manual on preaching. It covered every detail, down to how far the arms could be extended sideways from the body!

"Oh, and I must not forget to work on my basic Christian Library for Children," he reminded himself while sailing to Ireland, "much of which I have to either translate or condense."

Charles was angry when he heard about John's interest in Grace Murray from others. He had been completely open with John about Sally. To make matters worse for John, Grace had another suitor. And once again—just as with Sophy in America—John hesitated too long. Grace married the other suitor, one of the Methodist preachers! John was stung. Why had he waited too long again? It took a special meeting with Grace, her husband, and Charles to console John.

Only John's societies gave him joy. Here, he was living in Christ. When his sister Hetty died in London, John's only consolation was that his societies had brought her back to Christ.

So he labored tirelessly. But in early 1751 he

JOHN LABORED TIRELESSLY.

slipped on the ice on London Bridge and broke his ankle. Two friends took him to convalesce under the care of Molly Vazeille, a wealthy forty-year-old widow of a banker, the mother of grown children. John melted under her kind attention. "This time I will not hesitate," he told himself.

So at forty-seven he married Molly Vazeille. Charles, uninformed once again, refused to attend. Worse, John soon realized Molly had no sympathy for his life of travel. She wanted to know why John couldn't just settle down in London. He was widely respected now. The old days of mobs and violence were over.

John told her, "A Methodist preacher cannot answer to God if he preaches one sermon less or travels one day less in a married state than in a single state. Why not travel with me?"

So Molly tried to travel with him. But she was a rich woman, accustomed to luxury. Traveling with John was very hard. Soon their marriage was reduced to John seeing her in her own London home

MOLLY TRIED TO TRAVEL WITH JOHN.

only during the bitterest winter months. Molly was very resentful. Their marriage was a failure.

Before long, John had another problem. In November of 1753, he had preached in weather so cold he felt he was standing in ice water. Day after day he was drawn into situations that chilled him to the bones. Finally he returned to London with pain in his left lung, a racking cough, and a low fever. Soon he had a rattling cough.

A doctor urged him, "Go to bed at once!"

John had a dread infection called "galloping consumption." It was usually fatal. This moment was black for John, as bad as the worst storm at sea. Charles had drifted away from him. His wife was bitter. And now this disease. John was just fifty, with a thousand things left to do—but not dying. Was he afraid? How could he be? Paradise could come at any moment.

Ever methodical, he composed an epitaph for his tombstone, fearing someone else would write one too sentimental or too flattering. He reflected that before

HE COMPOSED AN EPITAPH FOR HIS TOMBSTONE.

his marriage he had renounced any claim on his wife's wealth. His personal wealth amounted to almost nothing. That pleased him very much!

"It is very important for a Methodist minister to die with almost nothing," he told himself.

At peace, he prayed for a while, and then he began to think. Obviously, the medications prescribed by his physician were not working. Now, if he were to use his own home medical book, what would he try?

He had a plaster made of sulfur and egg white on brown paper and had his left side wrapped. "God, help me, if it is Your will," he said hopefully. Five minutes later the pain in his lung was gone. In half an hour he had no fever. He was going to live.

It took several weeks to recover, but John was not idle. He condensed books for the Christian Library for Children.

To his sorrow, he learned his brother Charles's wife Sally and their only child, eighteen-month-old Jacky, named for John himself, caught smallpox. Then Jacky died. John now spent more time with

IT TOOK SEVERAL WEEKS TO RECOVER.

Charles than he had in many years. Charles was suffering profound grief.

John also learned his own near-fatal illness had shocked the societies. Every Methodist in England and Ireland was speculating on the question of leaving the Church of England if the Wesleys were not there to hold them to the church.

The 1755 conference at Leeds brought the question to the forefront. For three days, the sixty-three leaders discussed separating from the church. Many wanted to separate because of the hostility they encountered in their parish churches; some were even refused Holy Communion. John insisted that he wished to stay within the Church of England, but he also insisted that it was fully legal within church doctrine to field preach, to pray without the Book of Common Prayer, to form Methodist societies, and to allow preaching by those not ordained by bishops.

Then John concluded, "Before I will surrender any of those four activities I will quit the Church of England!"

THE LEADERS DISCUSSED SEPARATING FROM THE CHURCH.

Charles was enraged. He didn't want to ever leave the Church of England. He faithfully managed the Methodist center in Bristol, but by 1757 he no longer traveled at all.

Yet Methodism grew. By 1765, the societies embraced thirty-nine circuits administered by ninety-two preachers. Membership totaled over twenty thousand. Then the 1769 conference in Leeds took up what seemed a small order of business.

Some members of Methodist societies had emigrated to America. They wanted to keep their Methodism alive there. The conference members responded by sending two preachers to America. The new preachers soon reported that New York and Philadelphia each had one hundred members.

In 1770, John reflected on his health:

> *I can hardly believe that I am this day*
> *entered into the sixty-eighth year of my age.*
> *How marvelous are the ways of God! How*

SOME MEMBERS EMIGRATED TO AMERICA.

has He kept me even from a child! From ten to thirteen or fourteen, I had little but bread to eat, and not great plenty of that. I believe this was so far from hurting me, that it laid the foundation of lasting health. When I grew up. . .I chose to eat sparingly, and drink water. This was another great means of continuing my health. . . . (I) am now healthier than I was forty years ago. This hath God wrought!

"I AM NOW HEALTHIER THAN I WAS FORTY YEARS AGO."

"I MUST GO."

14

Death was never far away in the England of the 1700s. John's sister Sukey died in 1764, followed by his sister Emily in 1771. Of the once large family, only the two brothers and sisters Patty and Anne survived. Patty now lived at the Foundry. She had become a small part of the famous intellectual circle around Samuel Johnson. John met occasionally with Samuel Johnson, too, but the stay was always brief.

"You talk well on any subject," enthused Johnson. "Cross your legs and stay a while longer."

"Pardon me, sir, but I am obliged to meet with a widow and her family in an hour," explained John. "I must go."

"You are always in a hurry, sir," complained Johnson.

"No, sir. I am always in haste, but never in a hurry. I never undertake more than I can do with perfect calmness of spirit."

Of eight infants, Charles and Sally now had three children surviving. Charles Junior was fourteen, Sally twelve, and Sammy five. Both boys were musical prodigies, and Charles longed to have them study music in London. So Charles moved his family into a wealthy patron's four-story mansion in London. Although officially Charles helped pastor the chapels at the Foundry and West Street, it seemed to John that Charles had taken one more step away from Methodism.

Occasionally John reconciled with his wife Molly, but it never lasted. Molly had wealth, and she made it clear she needed John for nothing.

By 1771, the Methodists in America were still clamoring for preachers. How could they spread the gospel to an entire continent with just two preachers?

BOTH BOYS WERE MUSICAL PRODIGIES.

So John sent two more preachers to America, one of whom was twenty-six-year-old Francis Asbury. By the time the American Methodists held their first conference in Philadelphia in 1773, they numbered ten preachers and over eleven hundred members!

But as promising as America seemed now for Methodism, it also was ripe for turmoil. The colonists resented every intrusion by the king's authority. And King George the Third was determined to assert his authority. When the Americans declared their independence from England in 1776, war seemed inevitable. John had to urge his preachers to return to England. Only Francis Asbury stayed to tend the flock of seven thousand Methodists.

"What a shame if the Methodist societies in America were to perish!" cried John.

In England Methodism flourished. John laid the first stone for a new chapel off City Road. The City Road chapel would replace the Foundry—a Methodist center for nearly forty years.

John also realized with wonder that in forty

KING GEORGE WAS DETERMINED TO ASSERT HIS AUTHORITY.

years he had never been robbed on England's roads, and yet robbery on lonely stretches was common. "Can my safety be due to anything but the hand of God?" he asked.

John had been thrown by his horse or gone down with his fallen horse dozens of times, too. Finally, at seventy-five, his riding days ended. He was healthy but brittle. He now traveled by coach. When John's wife Molly died, he was so far away he did not get word until after her funeral. Many good friends died. But John was phenomenally durable. In his seventies he wrote:

> *My sight is considerably better now, and my nerves firmer, than they were (thirty years ago). . . . The grand cause is, the good pleasure of God, who doeth whatsoever pleaseth Him. The chief means are: 1. My constantly rising at four, for about fifty years. 2. My generally preaching at five in the morning, one of the most*

JOHN NOW TRAVELED BY COACH.

*healthy exercises in the world. 3. My never
traveling less, by sea or land, than four
thousand five hundred miles in a year.*

He had in fact become the respected old Methodist, even to the Church of England. After forty-five years of field preaching, he recorded:

*I preached at St. Thomas's church in
the afternoon, and at St. Swithin's in the
evening. The tide is now turned. . .I have
more invitations to preach in churches
than I can accept.*

Nevertheless, there was much anxiety among Methodists about his successor. If something wasn't done formally, the societies might bicker among themselves and disintegrate after he died. And the situation in America neared a crisis for fifteen hundred Methodists. England had lost the war. America was independent. The Church of England would offer no

ENGLAND HAD LOST THE WAR.

ordained clerics to give the American Methodists their needed sacraments. What then were the Methodists of America to do?

"Thousands of our American brothers and sisters cannot be baptized nor receive Holy Communion," said John in the conference of 1784.

So he ordained Thomas Coke the superintendent of Methodists in America. Coke would go to America and convene a conference. Then Coke would ordain ministers to give the sacraments.

John's next revelation was a plan to manage the societies after he passed on. This conference at Leeds would approve a constitution and set up a "Legal Hundred," the body of leaders that would govern the societies.

John still insisted Methodism in England was not a church. He would no longer say that about Methodism in America. That Christmas the American Methodists met in Baltimore to form an official Methodist Church. Coke revealed the mountain of material that John Wesley had given him to found the church:

THE AMERICAN METHODISTS MET IN BALTIMORE.

four volumes of John's *Sermons and Notes on the New Testament,* a service *Book of Worship* with liturgies, a *Book of Hymns* and a *Book of Discipline.* The *Book of Discipline* contained not the well-known thirty-nine Articles of the Church of England but twenty-five Articles that became the core of American Methodism, including one article that demanded allegiance to the American government!

Meanwhile, in London, John pushed his wiry body on, often courting ruin as he did in January of 1785:

> *The poor of the society. . .(needed)*
> *clothes, as well as food. So on this, and the*
> *four following days I walked through the*
> *town, and begged two hundred pounds,*
> *in order to clothe them that needed it*
> *most. But it was hard work as most of the*
> *streets were filled with melting snow,*
> *which often lay ankle deep; so that my*
> *feet were steeped in snow water nearly*

THE *BOOK OF DISCIPLINE* BECAME
THE CORE OF AMERICAN METHODISM.

from morning till evening.

His brother Charles was wearing out, but not in pain or suffering. He simply did less each day. A poet to the last, he mumbled his last verses to wife Sally, who recorded them:

Jesus, my only hope Thou art,
Strength of my failing flesh and heart.
Oh, could I catch a smile from Thee
And drop into eternity!

Charles passed on in March of 1788—at eighty years of age.

CHARLES PASSED ON IN MARCH OF 1788.

JOHN OBSERVED HIS EIGHTY-FOURTH BIRTHDAY.

15

The brothers' partnership had endured for almost sixty years. John observed his eighty-forth birthday in his journal with none of the pleasure of previous years:

> *I am not so agile as I was in times past. . .*
> *my sight is a little decayed. . .and [pain is] in*
> *my right shoulder and arm, which I impute*
> *partly to a sprain, and partly to rheumatism.*
> *I find likewise some decay in my memory,*
> *with regard to names and things.*

Nevertheless, John doggedly continued his rounds of

the societies. The congregations were enormous. It was obvious to John they did not expect to see him again. This was farewell.

He marveled at what was happening in England. Factories were springing up wherever there was plenty of water and coal. It seemed new machines were invented daily: steel-rolling, the cotton-spinning jenny, the steam engine. "Whether this age of machinery will be good or not I do not know," he admitted, "but God certainly placed our societies in these blossoming giants."

In March of 1791, John was eighty-seven. He had been sick in bed for several days. He hardly dared think what he had done in fifty years. He had traveled at least 200,000 miles on sea and land. He had preached over forty thousand sermons. And how many times had he traveled his triangle of Methodist centers in London, Bristol, and Newcastle? Fifty times? And how many passages across the sea to Ireland? Twenty-one, wasn't it? And how many Methodists were there now worldwide? Fifty thousand?

NEW MACHINES WERE INVENTED DAILY.

JOHN WESLEY

All righteous, too. Methodists practiced holiness, learned discipline, and reached into their pockets to help the poor.

John tried to rise from bed. He couldn't. How often had he seen the dying unable to do anything but sing praise? Surely God would let him do the same. John sang:

> *I'll praise my Maker while I've breath,*
> *And when my voice is lost in death,*
> *Praise shall employ my nobler pow'rs;*
> *My days of praise shall ne'er be past,*
> *While life, and thought, and being last,*
> *Or immortality endures.*

He reassured those at his bedside, "The best of all is, God is with us." He had nothing to do now but close his eyes and praise God until the beginning of paradise.

"THE BEST OF ALL IS, GOD IS WITH US."

AWESOME BOOKS FOR KIDS!

The Young Reader's Christian Library
Action, Adventure, and Fun Reading!

This series for young readers ages 8 to 12 is action-packed, fast-paced, and Christ-centered! With exciting illustrations on every other page following the text, kids won't be able to put these books down! Over 100 illustrations per book. All books are paperbound. The unique size (4 ⅛" x 5 ⅜") makes these books easy to take anywhere!

A Great Selection to Satisfy All Kids!